DOWN-
HOME
TALK

DOWN-

An Outrageous Dictionary of

HOME

Colorful Country Expressions

TALK

•

DIANN SUTHERLIN SMITH
ILLUSTRATIONS BY ELWOOD H. SMITH

COLLIER BOOKS
Macmillan Publishing Company / New York

COLLIER MACMILLAN PUBLISHERS
London

Collier Books
Macmillan Publishing Company
866 Third Avenue, New York, NY 10022
Collier Macmillan Canada, Inc.

Library of Congress Cataloging-in-Publication Data
Smith, Diann Sutherlin.
    Down-home talk: an outrageous dictionary of colorful country
  expressions/Diann Sutherlin Smith: illustrations by Elwood
  Smith.
      p.   cm.
    ISBN 0-02-045041-9
    1. English language—Provincialisms—United States—Glossaries,
  vocabularies, etc.   2. English language—Terms and phrases.
  3. Figures of speech.   4. Americanisms.   5. Country life—United
  States—Terminology.   I. Sternbergh, Leslie.   II. Title.
  PE2839.S6   1988
  427'.973—dc19   88-9576   CIP

Macmillan books are available at special discounts for bulk
purchases for sales promotions, premiums, fund-raising, or
educational use. For details, contact:
    Special Sales Director
    Macmillan Publishing Company
    866 Third Avenue
    New York, NY 10022

10 9 8 7 6 5 4 3 2 1

Printed in the United States of America

To my parents, who taught me that life is short and full of blisters

PREFACE

When I was no bigger than the hammer on a twenty-two, I was fluent in the down-home language. Sunday dinner at my Grandmother Lillian's was a sort of Berlitz course. There were so many relatives you couldn't stir 'em with a stick—and they all ate like a bunch of field hands, according to my father. Poor Uncle Otis with his preoccupation with carburetors was crazy as a peach orchard boar. His hen-plump wife Marguerite was spread out like Dallas, but she had a heart as big as her behind. And when Maylon (my second cousin once removed) wheeled into the gravel drive in his salmon-and-white, finned Plymouth, it was generally exclaimed that he had enough money to burn a wet mule.

It was not until many years after those sticky Sundays in front of the oscillating fan that I came to understand that not everyone spoke my language. Indeed, many folks were downright bewildered by my seemingly bizarre turn of descriptive phrase. It was then that I came to truly appreciate the beauty of down-home talk and started to collect and preserve many of these wonderful, surreal expressions.

To all those friends, relatives and colorful acquaintances whose contributions helped make this volume possible, my heartfelt thanks. You've made me happier than a dead hog in the sunshine.

—Diann Sutherlin Smith
Little Rock, Arkansas

DOWN-HOME TALK

AGE

Old as black pepper.

Old as dirt.

Old as God.

He has so many wrinkles he has to screw his hat on.

Her face has more wrinkles than a washboard.

I've been around the pot after the handle longer than you.

Haven't seen you in a coon's age.

ANGER

Mad as fire.

Mad as a puffed toad-frog.

Mad as a rooster in an empty hen house.

Mad as a bear with a sore ass.

Madder than a wet settin' hen.

Mad and swole up like a poisoned pup.

Madder than a sore-titted bitch.

Mad enough to throw a hissy fit.

Mad enough to spit nails.

Mad enough to spit nails.

Mad enough to see brass gnats.

Mad enough to take a dip of snuff.

So angry he can't spit straight.

So mad he was spittin' worse than a goose.

Got sand in his gizzard.

That makes my rear want to dip snuff.

I told him how the cow ate the cabbage.

I'm gonna cloud up and rain all over you.

I'm gonna whup knots on your head faster than you can rub 'em!

I'm fixin' to dot your eyes.

4

Toppin' the timber.

Kickin' up stumps.

Go soak your head in buttermilk!

APPEARANCES

All vine and no taters.

All hat and no cattle.

You can't tell by lookin' at a toad how high he'll jump.

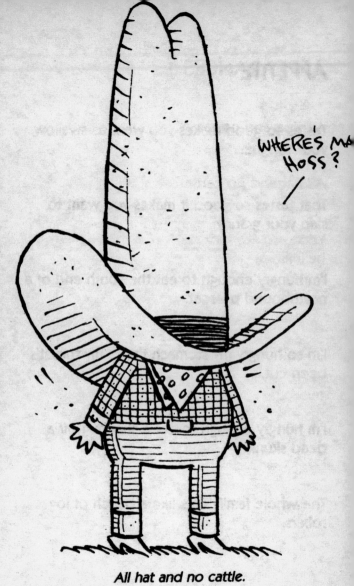

All hat and no cattle.

APPETITE

Tastes so good makes you want to swallow your tongue.

That tastes so good it makes you want to slap your granny.

I'm hungry enough to eat the south end of a northbound polecat.

I'm so hungry my stomach thinks my throat's been cut.

I'm hungry enough to eat a stinkbug off a dead skunk.

The whole family eats like a bunch of log rollers.

They eat like field hands.

I'm full as a tick.

BEAUTY

Cuter than a Junebug on a sow's ear.

Cuter than a speckled pup under a red wagon.

Built like a brick shithouse.

Pretty as a goggle-eyed perch.

Pretty enough to take to a barn dance.

Pretty as a goggle-eyed perch.

BUSY

Busy as bees in a barrel of molasses.

Busy as a coon in a roastin'-ear patch.

Busy as a long-nosed weevil in a cotton patch.

Busy as a one-legged man at an ass-kickin'.

Busy as a one-armed paper hanger.

Busy as a barefoot boy in an ant bed.

Busier than a swarm of dog peter gnats.

CLOTHING

He's dressed up like a mule in a buggy harness.

As sexy as socks on a rooster.

Her clothes fit tighter than a first-day bride's.

His suit fits like a family of gypsies just moved out.

His pants look like he's smugglin' rice out of China.

As sexy as socks on a rooster.

CLUMSY

He couldn't hit a bull in the ass with a bass fiddle.

He couldn't hit the ground if he fell.

His egg got shook.

He can't walk and chew tobacco at the same time.

COLD

Colder than a witch's tit in a brass brassiere.

Colder than a well-digger's ass in Idaho.

He couldn't hit a bull in the ass with a bass fiddle.

Cold enough to freeze the horns off a brass billy goat.

Cold as a gravestone in January.

COMMON

She's as common as pig's tracks.

Common as dishwater.

COMPLAINTS

You'd gripe if they hung you with a new rope.

If she went to heaven, she'd ask to see the upstairs.

What do you want—okra in your soup?

You'd gripe if they hung you with a new rope.

CONFUSION

Runnin' around like a chicken with its head cut off.

Runnin' around like a Junebug on a hot griddle.

Runnin' around like a cockroach in a hot skillet.

Like a rubber-nosed woodpecker in the Petrified Forest.

Twittle pated.

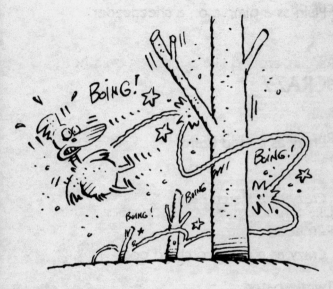

Like a rubber-nosed woodpecker in the Petrified Forest.

CONSPICUOUS

Stands out like a diamond in a goat's ass.

Plain as a pimple on a cheerleader.

CRAZY

Crazy as a road lizard.

Crazy as a March hare.

Crazy as a peach orchard boar.

Bat-brained.

Slap-assed crazy.

He don't know the meanin' of normal.

Crazy as a March hare.

CROWDED

So many folks you can't stir 'em with a stick.

Not enough room in here to cuss a cat.

So crowded you have to go outside to change your mind.

DARKNESS

Black as the inside of a cow.

Dark as pitch.

Dark as a stack of black cats.

DEPRESSION

So low he could wear a top hat and walk under a snake's belly.

So low you have to reach up to touch bottom.

My heart's heavier than a bucket of hog livers.

In low cotton.

Been down so long it looks like up to me.

Lower than a mole's belly button on diggin' day.

So low he could wear a top hat and walk under a snake's belly.

DIFFICULTY

Hard as pushin' a noodle through a keyhole.

Hard as pickin' fly shit out of black pepper.

Harder than pushin' a wheelbarrow with rope handles.

Like tryin' to lick honey off a thorn tree.

Like shootin' pool with a well rope.

DISCIPLINE

Whipped on like a red-headed stepchild.

DISHONESTY

Slippery as a hog on ice.

More slippery than an eel in a barrel of snot.

So crooked he'd steal the pennies off a
dead man's eyes.

So crooked they'll have to screw him in the
ground to bury him.

Crooked as a barrel full of fishhooks.

Crooked as a live oak limb.

He'd steal flies from a blind spider.

Slicker than a greased pig.

He'd steal flies from a blind spider.

Sneaky as a sheep-killin' dog.

Slick as a baby's bottom.

So slick he'd hold his own in a pond full of eels.

He'd steal the chew of tobacco out of your mouth if you yawned.

Narrow between the eyes.

She lies like a rug.

He lies so much he has to get his wife to call the dog for him.

DRY

Dry as a powder house.

So dry the fish stirred up dust swimmin' upstream.

So dry I could spit cotton.

Drier than a popcorn fart.

Dry as a goat's butt in March.

DIMWITTED

If his brains were dynamite, he couldn't blow his nose.

If you put his brains in a bluebird, it'd fly backwards.

If you put his brain on a fork, it would look like BB shot rollin' down a four-lane highway.

Sneeze! Your brains are dusty.

His head is thick as Mississippi mud.

He's got a head full of stump water.

He doesn't have the sense God gave a goose.

An idea would bust his head wide open.

There's no light in the attic.

His pilot light went out.

An idea would bust his head wide open.

His roof ain't nailed on tight.

He has room to let upstairs.

His bread ain't done.

Dull as a widow woman's ax.

Dumb as a box of rocks.

Dumber than a barrel of hair.

So dumb he couldn't pound sand in a rat hole.

So dumb he couldn't scatter shit with a rake.

So stupid he couldn't roll rocks down a steep hill.

He doesn't know crap from wild honey.

He doesn't know "c'mere" from "sic'em."

He knows as much about that as a dog knows about Sunday.

He doesn't know if it's Tuesday or Christmas.

She doesn't know if she's washin' or hangin' out.

He couldn't grow pole beans in a pile of horse shit.

He could mess up a one-car funeral.

He couldn't organize a piss-off in a brewery.

He'd hold a fish underwater to drown it.

ENDINGS

That's all she wrote.

The opry ain't over 'til the fat lady sings.

EXCITEMENT

Feisty as a calf in clover.

She's so excited she has to walk sideways to keep from flyin'.

Excited as a spring lizard in a hen house.

FEELINGS

Feel like death warmed over.

Feel like I been sent for and couldn't come.

Feel like death warmed over.

Feel like I been sackin' wildcats and run out of sacks.

Feel like I been jerked through a knothole backwards.

Feel like I been rode hard and put up wet.

Feel like I been run over by a Mack truck.

Feel like I been chewed up and spit out.

Feel like a bastard at the family picnic.

FINE

Finer than frog's hair.

Finer than frog's hair.

FLASHY

More chrome than a Cadillac.

All lit up like Christmas.

Shiny as a new dime in a goat's butt.

FRECKLES

She has more freckles than a turkey egg.

He has more freckles than a dog has fleas.

FRUGALITY

So tight that when he grins, his pecker skins
back.

So tight that when he blinks his eyes, his toes curl.

So tight he can call his every dollar by its first name.

So tight he squeezes a dollar 'til the eagle hollers.

Tight as last winter's long johns.

So tight if you threw him in the river he wouldn't make a bubble.

So tight he wouldn't pay a dime to see the Resurrection.

She makes pancakes so thin they've just got one side.

So stingy she'd skin a gnat for its hide and tallow.

So cheap he wouldn't pay a nickel to see a pissant eat a bale of hay.

So cheap he couldn't pay a dime to see a pissant pull a freight train.

He'd squeeze a nickel 'til the buffalo poots.

FUTILITY

Pointless as whitewashin' horse manure and settin' it up on end.

Like pitchin' straws in the wind.

Like tryin' to sneak daylight past a rooster.

Like drivin' a swarm of bees through a snowstorm with a switch.

Like tryin' to nail Jello on a tree.

So cheap he wouldn't pay a nickel to see a pissant eat a bale of hay.

Like a bug arguin' with a chicken.

If frogs had wings they wouldn't bump their butts.

In a turkey's dream you can!

Got about as much chance as a grasshopper in a hen house.

About as much chance as a head without a chicken.

GAIT

Walks like he has a corncob up his rear.

Walks like he has a hitch in his git-along.

Like a bug arguin' with a chicken.

GENEROSITY

She has a heart soft as summer butter.

She has a heart as big as her behind.

HANDSHAKING

He shakes your hand like he's clubbin' a snake.

He shakes hands like he's pumpin' a well.

He has a handshake limp as a dishrag.

He shakes your hand like he's clubbin' a snake.

HAPPINESS

Happy as a blowfly on a pile of dog shit.

Happy as a dog in a slaughterhouse.

Happy as a possum in a cow carcass.

Happy as a toad-frog under a drippy faucet.

As happy as if I had good sense.

A grin as wide as a watermelon rind.

A grin from his ass to his eyebrows.

That really melts my butter.

Grinnin' like a barrel of possum heads.

A grin as wide as a watermelon rind.

Grinnin' like a donkey shittin' saw briers.

Grinnin' like a shit-eatin' cat.

Grinnin' like a baked possum.

HOMELINESS

Ugly as Death's grandma.

Ugly enough to vomit a buzzard.

Ugly as homemade soap.

Ugly as skunk cabbage.

Ugly as yesterday.

Ugly enough to gag a maggot.

Ugly as a shaved ape.

He was so ugly they took his funeral up an alley.

So ugly she'd make a freight train take a dirt road.

So ugly when he lays on the beach the tide won't come in.

He's so ugly his daddy had to tie a pork chop around his neck so the dog would play with him.

He's so ugly he has to whup his feet every night so they'll get in bed with him.

A nose so long he could suck the guts out of a pumpkin through a knothole.

Neck as long as a well rope.

I wouldn't take her to a dog fight—even if she had a chance to win.

His ears stick out like a taxi with both doors open.

So buck-toothed he can eat corn on the cob through a picket fence.

His hair looks like it was parted by a bolt of lightnin'.

His hair's so greasy it looks like he combed it with buttered toast.

She has a face like a tow sack of turnips.

His eyes are closer together than an earthworm's.

She looks like somethin' the dog dragged in and the cat wouldn't eat.

His hair looks like it was parted by a bolt of lightnin'.

He looks like he's been hit in the face with a wet squirrel.

She looks like she's been beat with an ugly stick.

HOT

Hot as the hinges of hell.

Hot as a June bride in a feather bed.

Hot as the hub of hell.

Hot as a depot stove.

INEXPERIENCE

He just fell off a turnip truck.

She cooks peas and turnips in the same pot.

INSIGNIFICANT

Like a popcorn fart in hell.

Like a fart in a whirlwind.

Doesn't amount to a hill of beans.

Piddly-shit.

Like a popcorn fart in hell.

INTOXICATION

Higher than a cat's back.

High as a peckerwood hole.

Higher than a hen's ass at a dead run.

So drunk he couldn't hit his ass with both hands.

Drunk as Cooter Brown.

So drunk he couldn't hit the ground with his hat.

Knee-walkin' drunk.

Stewed to the gills.

So drunk he couldn't hit the ground with his hat.

LAZINESS

So lazy he stops plowin' to fart.

Too lazy to say "sooie" if the hogs were eatin' him.

Too lazy to say "sooie" if the hogs were eatin' him.

So lazy he follows the shade around the house.

He was born lazy and had a setback.

He was born in the middle of the week and lookin' both ways for Sunday.

He's a good old dog but he don't like to hunt.

LIFE

Life is like bein' on a mule team. If you ain't the lead mule, all the scenery looks the same.

Life is short and full of blisters.

Life is just one damned thing after another.

Life is short and then you die.

Tomorrow's just the same soup, different bowl.

What goes 'round, comes 'round.

MEANNESS

Tough as a pine knot.

He's tougher than a tombstone.

Mean as a snake with an abscessed fang.

Mean as a crocodile with a gum boil.

Meaner than a junk yard dog.

Mean as a snake with an abscessed fang.

Mean enough to tear up an anvil.

Mean as cat crap.

NERVOUSNESS

So nervous she could thread a sewin' machine with it runnin'.

Jumpy as a basketful of bullfrogs.

Jumpy as a basketful of bullfrogs.

Nervous as a porcupine in a balloon factory.

Nervous as a long-tailed cat in a room full of rockers.

Nervous as a whore in church.

NOISE

Sang like her foot was caught in a bear trap.

A squeal like a stuck pig.

Noisier than two skeletons makin' love on a tin roof.

Quieter than a mouse pissin' on a cotton ball.

She couldn't carry a tune in a bucket with the lid on it.

A voice like a buzz saw on cast iron.

OBESITY

Fat as Aunt Eppie's prize hog.

Fat as a Poland-China sow.

Fat as a bale of cotton.

The back of her pants looks like a tow sack with two hogs rasslin' in it.

Spread out like Dallas.

When you tell her to haul ass, she has to make two trips.

She couldn't carry a tune in a bucket with the lid on it.

An ass as fat as a river bottom coon.

She's spread out like a cold supper.

A hen-plump woman.

Big enough to go bear huntin' with a switch.

POVERTY

Poor as gully dirt.

Dirt-dog poor.

So poor he couldn't put a down payment on a hot dog.

So poor he can't change his mind.

Poor as Job's turkey.

So poor she can't go window shoppin'.

So poor the bank won't let him draw breath.

Broker than the Ten Commandments.

Don't have a pot to piss in or a bed to shove it under.

Ground so poor it can't raise a flagpole.

PROCREATION

That mare's so inbred she's her own grandmother.

She's got enough kids to bait a trotline.

She has a whole passel of young 'uns.

They have kids from Widlum to Wadlum.

He's like a Missouri mule—no ancestry and no hope for posterity.

RELUCTANCE

Before I'd do that I'd get a tin beak and peck shit with the chickens.

I'd rather walk through an alley wearin' cheese underwear.

I'd as soon slap my momma.

RESIGNATION

Might as well, can't dance.

Before I'd do that I'd get a tin beak and peck shit with the chickens.

SALESMANSHIP

He couldn't sell whores in a lumber camp.

SCARCITY

Scarce as hog tracks on a linen tablecloth.

Scarce as horse manure in a two-car garage.

Scarce as hen's teeth.

SKINNY

She looks like a red worm with the shit flung out of it.

So thin she could bathe in a gun barrel.

If he turns sideways and sticks out his tongue, he looks like a zipper.

He has to stand up twice to cast a shadow.

He's a long, tall drink of water.

Skinnier than a bar of soap after a hard day's wash.

Thinner than a bat's ear.

Scarce-hipped.

She's no bigger than the hammer on a twenty-two.

So skinny you have to shake the sheets to find her.

So skinny you could paint stripes on her and use her for a yardstick.

No bigger than a minute.

So thin he only has one side.

SLOW

So slow you have to set up stakes to see if he's movin'.

So slow he couldn't catch the seven-year itch.

Too slow to catch a cold.

Slow as molasses in January.

If they hang me, I hope they send you after the rope.

Quick as a herd of turtles.

So thin she could bathe in a gun barrel.

SOPHISTICATION

Slick as a Philadelphia lawyer.

SPEED

Like a bat out of Georgia.

Like a bat out of hell.

Fast as an Arkansas preacher can spot a counterfeit nickel.

Faster than an alligator can chew a puppy.

Faster than a scalded dog.

Get on it like a fat lady on a milkshake.

Faster than a scalded dog.

Quicker than greased lightnin'.

I can do that in a whipstitch.

STRENGTH

So strong he can crunch pecans between his toes.

SURPRISE

Well, I'll be a suck-egg mule!

Well, shoot me a-runnin'!

Well, drag me in the bushes and leave me for ripe!

Well, slap me naked and hide my clothes!

That takes the rag off the bush!

Now if that don't beat all!

TALKATIVE

An empty wagon rattles the loudest.

Her tongue is tied in the middle and waggin' at both ends.

She has a tongue like a bell clapper.

He can talk tomatoes off the vine.

He can cuss a gate off its hinges.

He can talk tomatoes off the vine.

TORRENTIAL RAINS

Frog strangler.

Gully washer.

Toad drowner.

It rained like a cow pissin' on a flat rock.

Sod soaker.

TROUBLE

She got her tit caught in the wringer.

He's up to his ears in hornets.

He really crapped in the oatmeal this time.

He's in a bad row of stumps.

He really pissed in the whiskey.

TRUTH

Don't be pissin' down my back and tellin' me it's rainin'.

If I tell you a rooster dips snuff, you can look for the can under his wing.

If I tell you Santa Claus is comin', you better hang up your sock.

Is a pig's ass pork?

He really crapped in the oatmeal this time.

You ain't just whistlin' Dixie.

He'd rather tell a lie on credit than the truth for cash.

VANITY

I wish I could buy her for what she's worth and sell her for what she thinks she's worth.

She wouldn't go to a funeral unless she could be the corpse.

Her nose is so high in the air she'd drown in a rainstorm.

Proud as a dog with two tails.

Proud as a four-horned billy goat.

Proud as a dog with two tails.

WEAKNESS

He's got the guts of a butterfly.

WEALTH

He has more money than Quaker has oats.

More money than a porcupine has quills.

He's got enough money to burn a wet mule.

Richer than six inches up a bull's ass.

She's puddlin' in tall cotton.

Stiff in the heels.

WELCOME

About as welcome as a polecat at a camp meetin'.

WORTHLESS

Useless as tits on a boar hog.

Worthless as a fork in a bowl of soup.

Worthless as a pinch of sour owl manure.

Worthless as a dead possum tail.

Worthless as a milk bucket under a bull.

Worthless as cold snail tracks.

Worthless as bumps on a side of bacon.

Ain't worth dried spit.

You need that like a pig needs a side
saddle.

Handier than hip pockets in a shroud.

He ain't fit to carry guts to a bear.

Like a tomcat needs a weddin' license.

Sorry as a lope-headed bird dog.

DID I MISS SOMETHING?

Well, don't get madder than a tied-up coon if your favorite down-home expressions got left out. Write them down and send them to me:

Diann Sutherlin Smith
c/o Collier Books
Macmillan Publishing Company
866 Third Avenue
21st Floor
New York, NY 10022

Your comments and contributions are as welcome as flowers in spring.